DEVELOP AND DELIVER
EFFECTIVE
PRESENTATIONS

A 10-step process to plan, practice, and rehearse a presentation on any business topic

BY NATASHA TERK

A self-paced training program for people in business

Write It Well

Corporations, professional associations, and other organizations may be eligible for special discounts on bulk quantities of Write It Well books and training courses. For more information, call (510) 655-6477 or email info@writeitwell.com.

Publisher:

> Write It Well
> PO Box 13098
> Oakland, CA 94661
>
> (510) 868-3322
>
> writeitwell.com

Author: Natasha Terk

Editor: Christopher Disman

To order this book, visit our website, writeitwell.com.

Publications by Write It Well include the following books, e-books, and e-learning modules from The Write It Well Series on Business Communication:

Professional Writing Skills

Effective Email: Concise, Clear Writing to Advance Your Business Needs

Reports, Proposals, and Procedures

Land the Job: Writing Effective Resumes and Cover Letters

Writing Performance Reviews

Write It Well offers a variety of customized on-site and online training courses, including the following courses:

Effective Email

Professional Writing Skills

Writing Performance Reviews

Writing Resumes and Cover Letters

Technical Writing

Marketing and Social Media Writing

Management Communication Skills

Global Teamwork and Meeting Skills

Presentation Skills

Reports, Proposals, and Procedures

Train-the-trainer kits are also available to accompany these courses.

We offer coaching to improve individual professionals' writing and presenting skills. We also offer editorial, layout, and writing services to help individual authors and teams send out well-organized documents in language that's correct, clear, concise, and engaging.

For more information about any of our content or services,

- Visit writeitwell.com
- Email us at info@writeitwell.com
- Or give us a call at (510) 868-3322

CONTENTS

INTRODUCTION

Characteristics of effective speakers

At Write It Well, we see communication as a core business skill. Delivering presentations is an important part of many people's jobs — especially as you advance in seniority. And most people's jobs involve sharing ideas; updating coworkers, clients, or customers; and suggesting solutions to business problems.

Anyone can tackle these spoken-communication challenges, either formally or informally. A professional presentation is simply a formal, prepared speech that advances the business needs of both a presenter and a given audience.

It can be tricky to deliver any presentation. Many of us aren't sure where to begin, how to plan what we'll say, or how to prepare for the actual presentation day. Effective speakers plan their presentations thoroughly and then carefully practice how they'll deliver their ideas. The techniques in this book will show you how to develop a solid presentation plan and then put the plan into practice through effective presentation delivery.

The professional stakes may be low or high for your next business presentation. Planning and practice will help you match any presentation to the area of overlap between your own communication needs and the communication needs of your audience. Investing time and energy into your presentation skills can also make you much more effective in the long term — as a team member, team leader, or entrepreneur.

The importance of planning and practice

Presenters often start out by focusing on what information *they* need to share with the audience. However, it's much more helpful to start out the other way around: by asking yourself what information *the audience* needs to hear.

Putting the audience first can help minimize any professional nervousness you feel. Namely, you can worry less about how you'll look by focusing more on how you'll help other people grasp larger business ideas.

PLANNING makes any presentation more effective. Collecting, organizing, and formatting content are crucial to help an audience understand your information. The planning process develops a clear outline that you're ready to fill in on the day you speak.

After the developmental planning process, it's also crucial to practice **DELIVERING** your presentation. The mechanics of your speech boil down to how you'll look, speak, and move, and also ask and answer questions. Considering all these factors helps you feel confident that your audience will be able to follow you.

Posing questions to prepare your speech

Public speaking can give almost all of us butterflies in our stomachs. If you feel any butterflies, think of them as questions you'll need to answer. For instance …

- Who am I speaking to?
- Why am I speaking in the first place?
- How should I articulate all my ideas?
- How do I organize [**X**] minutes' or hours' worth of thoughts?
- How do I interact with the audience to really involve them in what I'm saying?
- What's the right kind of eye contact?
- What are the best ways to use my voice?
- How will I look if I move or don't move as I speak?
- How do I answer audience questions?
- How do I reach out to people in an engaging way but also keep us all strictly on time?

That's ten questions, and they represent a lot of potential butterflies! However, you're certain to become a much more effective speaker simply by asking these kinds of questions and answering them methodically. This book will help you answer every question above.

Planning and practicing your presentation

Here are a few challenges that effective presenters overcome when they develop a presentation plan and practice delivering it:

- Deciding what information a particular audience needs to hear
- Settling on a main point and an organizational strategy
- Formatting information in a style that works well for that audience
- Using their eyes, voices, and body language to engage with the audience
- Rehearsing ways to manage everyone's time effectively

Knowing that you've weighed these topics can help you stay firmly focused on your ideas when your time comes to speak. When you follow a clearly planned sequence of ideas, your audience will have a much easier time following you — leaving everyone satisfied at the end of your presentation.

This book will guide you through two five-step planning processes. First, you'll develop a careful presentation plan in five steps. Then you'll follow five more steps to practice successfully delivering your well-planned set of messages to your audience.

THINK ABOUT IT …

Think about presenters you've seen. What impression do you usually form when they …

- Show more interest in their topics than in audience members' reactions?
- Ramble on without getting to the point?
- Look at the ground or the ceiling while they speak?
- Speak with their backs to the audience?
- "Um" and "uh" their ways through a speech?
- Slouch?
- Present with their arms folded across their chests?

SIMULTANEOUSLY PREPARE A SPEECH AND GROW AS A PROFESSIONAL

Strengthening your presentation skills is a dramatic way to advance your career. This course also includes further tools toward your career development — activities that you'll practice automatically as you prepare for your next presentation.

This course suggests a variety of ways you can consciously link your presenting skills with your leadership, teamwork, project management, problem-solving, analytical, and other core professional abilities. Also see other books in The Write It Well Series on Business Communication (e.g., *Professional Writing Skills* and *Reports, Proposals, and Procedures*) for further career-development suggestions.

EXERCISE

Here are some questions to help you articulate your own values about public speaking as a form of skilled business communication. Think about these values during this book's pair of five-step planning and delivery processes.

What qualities are important to you when you *listen* to a good or bad presentation?

What qualities stand out when you *watch* a good speaker?

And what qualities do you find *distracting* during a presentation?

PART ONE:
DEVELOP YOUR PRESENTATION

Objectives
. . . .

Here are some of the planning challenges you'll master in Part One:

- Identify how your audience usually processes information
- Decide whether your main purpose is to inform your audience, or to persuade them to do something
- Articulate your message in effective language
- Figure out ways to organize your ideas so they'll be clear to you and clear to your audience

All these actions will help you develop a solid presentation that's clear in your mind and easy for your audience to follow.

Here are Part One's five steps to develop your presentation:

- **Step 1. Identify your audience**
- **Step 2. Identify your purpose and most important message**
- **Step 3. Use notes to articulate your ideas**
- **Step 4. Organize your notes**
- **Step 5. Plan an in-person or virtual presentation**

You'll find explanations of each step below.

Step 1. Identify your audience

Identify how your audience usually processes information

Start out by looking at your central presentation topic from your listeners' point of view. If you don't have a central topic yet, then run through these three steps:

- Think about your listeners
- Think about your expertise
- Identify a topic that represents an overlap between what you know and what's likely to engage your listeners

Your audience members may have different backgrounds, interests, needs, concerns, or levels of technical knowledge. Here are some questions to answer about your audience members:

- **WHAT DO THEY ALREADY KNOW ABOUT MY TOPIC?** For example, if many listeners won't be familiar with your topic at all, then you might plan to include some history or background information in your introduction. If all listeners *will* be familiar with your basic topic, then look for ways to present it in a new light or emphasize aspects of it that will be new to them.

- **HOW INTERESTED ARE LISTENERS IN THE SUBJECT?** Are they already interested, or are you hoping that your presentation will build interest?

- **HOW WILL THEY USE MY INFORMATION?** Perhaps a few listeners will use your information to implement a project plan. They may therefore need detailed information. Meanwhile, all of your other listeners may need a 45-minute overview of the project status. In this case, you might plan your presentation as a one-hour talk centering on a project overview that will concern everyone. You could leave a few minutes near the end to address the topic of implementation, and prepare a handout for the small group of listeners who need that further information. You could then arrange a time to address or write to these audience members separately.

- **WHY WILL THEY LISTEN — I.E., WHAT'S IMPORTANT TO THEM?** What will motivate audience members to pay attention? What kinds of business needs do they usually act on? What professional concerns or goals do they have?

- **WHAT DO THEY NEED TO LEARN?** What kind of information will not be familiar? What information may sound strange?

UNDERSTAND YOUR AUDIENCE TO GROW AS A PROFESSIONAL LEADER

Presentations may seem like a somewhat advanced professional skill, but practicing for just one presentation can also represent a longer-term investment in your career. Many of the challenges in this book translate into solid professional development—starting with an effort to understand your audience. This single process offers automatic professional returns on your investment of time and energy, for a specific presentation and beyond:

- Understanding different audiences will make you a more effective business writer in many situations.
- Engaging in this process can help you motivate your colleagues or team members on other occasions.
- It can prepare you to coach or mentor colleagues who don't have your professional expertise in different areas.
- And it can help you appreciate that it's important to tailor a professional message to its specific recipients. Many managerial and executive roles involve recognizing the interests and needs of very different listeners or readers.

EXERCISE

Think of a presentation that you need to develop and deliver, and answer each of the following questions to identify your audience. Use your computer or some notepaper to record your answers.

- **What do they already know about my topic?**

- **How interested are they in my subject?**

- **How will they use my information?**

- **Why will they listen?**

- **What do they already know?**

- **What's important to them?**

Decide on a tone to match your audience and the occasion

Think consciously about what mood your presentation should have as a whole. How will the audience probably feel about your topic? What kind of mood do you hope to end with?

Here are the kinds of questions that will help you plan effectively:

- Should your presentation be entirely serious?
- Or is it appropriate to be light-hearted and plan a few jokes?
- When listeners are engaged in an activity, should they feel serious — e.g., for a safety-related topic?
- Or should they feel amused — e.g., for a game that develops a skill but also builds camaraderie and teamwork?

Here are some specific "On the one hand ..." and "On the other hand ..." considerations that you may need to balance to strike the right tone:

- Sounding formal enough yet casual enough
- Sounding confident but not superior
- Sounding authoritative yet open to new information

Be careful if you deliberately aim to convey emotions — especially anger or other negative emotions. It's usually best to leave participants room to have their own emotional reactions to your content as you aim for an engaged, supportive, yet professionally neutral tone.

You may need to develop a presentation that includes or focuses on a sensitive topic. Here are three rules of thumb for sensitive messages:

- Stick to the facts
- Use neutral language
- Avoid embarrassing anyone in the audience

Finally, here's a checklist of eight traits shared by most effective business speakers:

- ☐ They balance self-respect with respect for the audience
- ☐ They show sensitivity for audience members' feelings
- ☐ They speak to help others develop, rather than to hear their own voices
- ☐ They show reliable knowledge of the business topic
- ☐ They share enthusiasm without letting it carry them away
- ☐ They are open to different points of view
- ☐ They display inexhaustible patience
- ☐ They have an appropriate sense of humor

Note any traits above that you think you might find difficult. If finding the right tone feels like a delicate balancing act, then use this checklist as a guide for the tone you'll aim to strike and the image you'll aim to project. Developing all these traits in yourself will help you weave the right tone into the fabric of your presentation.

EXERCISE

Take a minute to describe what tone you'll use to address your audience. Look again at the checklist above and decide whether any particular trait may be a challenge for you. If so, make a note for yourself.

_____

_____

_____

_____

_____

_____

_____

Step 2. Identify your purpose and most important message

Prepare a key sentence that expresses your most important message

You're probably familiar with key sentences for business writing. Key sentences can be just as helpful in a presentation to deliver your most important idea.

Your key sentence is a kind of elevator pitch: the concise idea you'd say to an important contact when the elevator doors might close at any moment.

What would you shout if you had 15 seconds to get your most important message across to someone who could help you accomplish some shared business goals? What if you had just five seconds? Those questions will help you arrive at your presentation's key sentence.

EXERCISE

Use your computer or some notepaper to write out your key sentence. Then rephrase the sentence in two or three different ways.

Look for words that you'll feel comfortable saying. Then you'll be ready to practice restating your key message in several ways. Also picture your listeners' reactions to the key sentence, and make a note of what range of reactions you can anticipate.

_____

_____

_____

_____

_____

_____

_____

_____

_____

_____

Decide on your central purpose: to inform or to persuade

Have you ever listened to a presentation and felt confused about what the speaker's purpose was? Or have you attended a presentation but had a hard time afterward explaining the upshot of the speech to someone who wasn't there?

A presentation tends to get much more clear when the speaker makes an either/or decision about its main purpose:

- To **persuade** listeners to do something
- To give them **information**

You'll find that any presentation is a more effective communication tool when you know exactly what you want to accomplish by speaking: either to persuade, or to inform.

Here are some potential topics for when you need to **INFORM** your audience:

- Answer a question that listeners are likely to have
- Pose a question they probably haven't thought of
- Elaborate on information that listeners are somewhat familiar with
- Make your opinion known

Here are some potential topics for a presentation meant to **PERSUADE** your audience:

- Convince listeners to take action
- Persuade them to change their thinking and share your point of view
- Sell something
- Ask for help

And here's an illustration of how the same topic could be cast as one presentation to persuade an audience and could then be recast as a second presentation, later on, to inform the same audience:

TO PERSUADE:

March 2014: Call on your audience members to make donations so that a specific, positive action will become possible.

TO INFORM:

March 2015: Show your appreciation for past donations by explaining what specific, positive action became possible because of the audience members' donations in March 2014.

EXERCISE

Decide whether this speaker's main purpose is to inform or to persuade.

"Thank you again for your efforts in increasing sales. Now that we've accomplished this goal, we need to focus on cutting expenditures. Our marketing budget for next quarter has been cut by 25 percent, so we need to come up with ideas for doing more with less. We'll dedicate next week's meeting to discussing this issue. Please come prepared with your ideas."

☐ **INFORM**   ☐ **Persuade**

The speaker's main purpose in the example above is to persuade the audience members to prepare ideas to share at the meeting next week.

EXERCISE

Take a minute now to identify the central purpose of the presentation that you're developing.

_____

_____

_____

_____

IDENTIFY YOUR PURPOSE IN A VARIETY OF PROFESSIONAL ROLES

Here's another area of automatic overlap between presentations and general professional development. Team members and leaders always communicate more effectively when they identify their primary purpose for each agenda item in a meeting and each email, letter, or report they prepare. TEAM LEADERS often need to communicate a clear vision — e.g.,

- To give team members precise information
- To persuade them of the importance of an activity and persuade them to take action
- Or to pass on clear instructions

TEAM MEMBERS also need to have a clear grasp on the purpose of their meeting contributions, emails, and reports. A team often works more effectively when its members highlight a shared purpose — e.g.,

- By explaining they need further information
- By providing clear, informative progress updates
- Or by persuasively suggesting possible courses of action

Consciously identifying your purpose for a formal presentation can make it easier to identify your purpose for your everyday professional communication. Making it a habit to ask, "What's my purpose?" can make you a more efficient, effective, and influential professional communicator.

Identify and answer listeners' most important questions

You've already identified who will be in your audience. Next, think about your presentation's subject from the point of view of your audience members.

EXERCISE

Use your computer or some notepaper to write down all the questions your audience members might have. If you can picture someone asking you a question, then make a note of it.

This is a brainstorming process. Don't stop to evaluate or organize questions as you write them down: you'll do that in the next section.

_____

_____

_____

_____

_____

_____

_____

_____

_____

_____

_____

_____

Start with *audience members'* likely questions, instead of the answers that *you've* already assembled. That way, you'll focus on the information that your audience members need — not just the information that you'll enjoy talking about.

This kind of planning is one key to a successful presentation. This planning step makes it more likely that you'll persuade listeners to take action, or more likely that they'll retain the information you pass on.

MAKE YOUR HARD WORK EASY TO FOLLOW

You may have worked very hard to gather information, but don't confuse the value of your efforts with the value the information will have for your audience. Carefully considering audience members' needs is the best way to make sure your information will shine.

As you'll see, listeners' questions help you determine what information to include, and they suggest ways to organize your information so it's as easy as possible to follow.

Group related questions and answer them

Once you've brainstormed a list of all likely and unlikely questions, you're ready to start looking for patterns.

EXERCISE

Use this space or some note paper to write down all the questions your audience members might have. Follow these steps:

1. Identify related questions and group them together.
2. Cross out any unnecessary or repeated questions.
3. Briefly answer the overall questions. If the answer to a question is lengthy or if you don't have all the details, simply indicate what information will be most important to include in the time you'll have to speak.
4. Arrange your new question-and-answer sets in the most logical order.

_____

_____

_____

_____

_____

_____

_____

_____

_____

_____

Step 3. Use notes to articulate your ideas

Use paper or electronic notes to brainstorm — capturing every point that advances your presentation's central purpose

This process works whether you prefer notecards from the drugstore, the Apple Stickies app, or the Windows Sticky Notes program. Any of these methods can turn a floor, tabletop, physical desktop, or computer desktop into a space to jot down ideas for your presentation.

Whether your notes are paper or digital, use them to record your ideas. *Capturing* and *separating* each important idea is your focus at this stage:

1. If an idea is too long for one note, then break it up into several notes and put them side by side.

2. Start with the questions and answers you identified earlier. Add notes that clarify questions the audience is likely to have, and write out nearby notes with details that answer those questions.

3. Don't edit your thoughts at this stage. Just let your ideas flow, and worry about organizing them and prioritizing them later on.

Identify stories or examples that illustrate your points

One way to engage an audience is to tell stories that illustrate your ideas — for instance, an anecdote that proves a point or a vivid illustration of a general idea.

Your presentation will be more engaging if you space out a few illustrative stories, telling them after you've established your main theme and before you're ready to conclude.

Writing out story ideas on notes makes it easy to move the stories around to plan the best timing and best effect.

EXERCISE

On your computer or in your workspace, write out notes for one or more major topics your presentation should include:

1.   Think how you can illustrate at least one idea with a story

2.   Write the story idea on a note

3.   Place the story note beside the related idea

Arrange your notes in groups, setting aside notes that don't advance your purpose

You've already grouped your questions together, and that grouping action should suggest a natural logical grouping for your notes. Remember to put yourself in your audience members' shoes and arrange your ideas to be user-friendly for them.

Take these five steps if you think you have too many notes for your allotted time:

• Identify the most important groups of notes
• Ask yourself if each group advances your primary purpose
• Set aside any group of ideas that does *not* advance your presentation's purpose
• If any of those nonessential groups contains a crucial idea, then look for another group that can encompass that same idea
• If the idea doesn't fit under a major theme, then try to set the idea firmly aside and communicate with others about it in another way, at another time — not during your presentation

**DELETE A NOTE AND CONGRATULATE YOURSELF
ON A PROBLEM SOLVED**

It can feel painful to apply the words *redundant* and *unnecessary* to ideas that are valuable to you. But this selection process represents PROBLEM SOLVING, a core professional ability. A frequent business problem is deciding whether an idea is relevant, off topic, or not important enough to include in your current message — spoken or written.

Professional people rarely have time to spare, and overcrowding your message will waste their time. Wasted time is a very big problem. You'll successfully solve many communication challenges by omitting ideas in the planning stage. Respecting your listeners' time will boost their trust in you as a professional who's worth listening to.

Decide on one unifying theme for each note group

To start identifying presentation themes, look for patterns in your notes that will help you meet these three communication challenges:

- Introduce your topic to your audience
- Help them understand your main point and lesser points
- Grasp the messages that you want them to take away from your presentation

Keep yourself in the shoes of your audience members as you organize your groups of notes, and give each group a title so that it becomes a presentation theme. Here are six strategies that are often useful to organize business presentation themes in ways that audiences can easily follow:

- Chronological order
- Comparisons and contrasts
- Problem and solution
- Cost, size, and special features
- Past history, present status, and future projection
- Production efficiencies, decreased workloads, and cost savings

Identify themes that are well suited to the groups of ideas you've now developed.

Narrow down your presentation
to no more than three or four themes

Aim for no more than three or four major themes for a presentation, even if it's an all-day event. The longer your presentation is, the more narrowly you can subdivide each of its major themes.

If you don't have enough material to fill up your allotted time, then look for logical ways you can explore the ramifications of one topic. If the topic on one note could naturally branch out in two or three directions, then you'll have a naturally organized pair or trio of topics to fill the audience's time with useful information.

If you have too much material for your presentation's timeframe, then look for ways to consolidate and streamline your ideas. It can be easy to start feeling attached to an idea, and winnowing large or small ideas out of your presentation may feel painful.

But a note is only a note! A group of ideas that relate to your business concerns could always become the basis for a separate presentation. If a note or theme represents a valuable aspect of your business, then lay it aside while you're focused on this presentation. After your successful presentation, you can always turn a valuable note into a separate business email, conversation, or both.

Ruthlessly sticking to the point tends to pay off in a laser-focused presentation. The more streamlined your presentation is, the easier it will be for your listeners to follow. The easier your presentation is to follow, the more receptive your audience members will be to listening to you discuss other topics at another time.

EXERCISE

Follow the last few steps for the notes, note groups, and themes of your presentation. List the final three or four themes in the order you'll present them.

_____

_____

_____

_____

_____

_____

_____

Format your slides

Advanced formatting and features are complicated for PowerPoint, Apple's Keynote, and other presentation programs. But make sure any presentation includes at least the following simple slides:

- A title slide
- An agenda

Your agenda should follow the organizational structure you've already mapped out. Separate slides should announce each new theme, and font size and formatting should reflect what level of topic you're addressing at any moment: a major theme, a large group of ideas, or a smaller topic.

Also consider adding the following:

- A creative opening slide that's relevant to your topic and appropriate for your audience
- Slides to announce planned breaks or lunches
- A thank-you slide at the end

Step 4. Organize your notes

Weave your themes into an organic whole

You've identified three or four major themes now. This is a good time to step back and look at the forest as well as the trees. Return to four frameworks that you've already mapped out:

- Your overarching agenda
- Your key sentence (with a few ways to rephrase it several times)
- Your purpose in speaking: to persuade audience members, or to inform them
- The questions audience members will have

If you feel as if your presentation lacks focus, then reexamine your note groups in light of those four frameworks. They should map out a terrain where your own business purpose meshes with questions that your audience may have. Your strategies to rephrase your key sentence can also keep your presentation grounded as you advance through your agenda.

When you keep all these frameworks in place, a mass of notes will collectively take shape to bring a bigger picture into focus. Sound planning helps you achieve this focus well before you're scheduled to deliver your ideas.

MANAGE A PROJECT OR ANALYZE DATA

Organizing your ideas is a helpful process for many professional activities — e.g., **project management.** Clear categories of ideas can give you an overview of all the project details you need to track and complete, grouped by deadlines and types of activity. This kind of mental selection and rearrangement is also an **analytical** process, and analysis is another core ability that's often very useful in professional life.

Grouping your project details into categories can help you manage complexity, stay on schedule, and not lose sight of the forest for the trees. And clear spoken communication between team members and leaders is often vital to keep a project on track.

Find effective language

USE THE S3 TECHNIQUE

Three words that start with the letter *S* provide a great framework for turning your notes into a speaking plan or a full-blown script:

1. **STATE** your idea
2. **SUPPORT** it with further details
3. **SUMMARIZE** the point the audience should grasp

EXERCISE

Look for a note you've written for an idea that you aren't sure how to express. Use the S3 technique to write out a script to express that idea:

1. **STATE:**

2. **SUPPORT:**

3. **SUMMARIZE:**

USE CONCISE LANGUAGE

Listeners find it difficult to pay attention to long-winded language, so look for concise ways to express each idea you have. For instance, key words are often more effective than complete sentences on a slide.

Focused language has a bigger impact, so resist the temptation to speak at length to reinforce any point. Here are some examples of long-winded and concise language:

LONG-WINDED:
We <u>are in agreement</u> with you about the contract terms.

CONCISE:
We <u>agree</u> with you about the contract terms.

LONG-WINDED:
There was an invoice with the number of 1000000 — which, it transpires, was in the amount of $30,250.75, and this invoice had two credits that had been applied to it. I will state the amounts of these two credits. First, C-100001 amounted to $250.00, while, second, C-100002 amounted to $150.00.

CONCISE:
Invoice #1000000 amounted to $30,250.75. Two credits had been applied to it. C-190128 amounted to $250.00, while C-190215 amounted to $150.00.

USE ACTIVE LANGUAGE

One strategy to keep your speech precise is to focus on the verbs — the words that convey the dynamic actions of a sentence.

As you can see in the following examples of active language, the actor comes before the verb. To use active language, say *who* acts, not just what the action is. The actor is underlined in the following revisions, and the action is boldfaced.

PASSIVE	The project **was managed** by <u>John</u>.
ACTIVE	<u>John</u> **managed** the project.

(unnecessary words: "was" and "by") (actor: <u>John</u>)
(action: managed)

PASSIVE	The system **has been checked** by <u>me</u> for the IPs that

were found by <u>you</u> to
have been missing.

ACTIVE	<u>I</u> **checked** the system for the IPs that <u>you</u> **found**

were missing.

When you give instructions, it's particularly important to say clearly what you want your listeners to do. It can be frustrating and confusing to try to follow instructions in passive language.

PASSIVE	The IPs **should be checked** and **confirmed** by <u>the end users</u>.
ACTIVE	<u>The end users</u> should **check** and **confirm** the IPs.

— OR —

Please **check** and **confirm** the IPs.
(an implied <u>you</u>, if the presenter were addressing end users in the
audience)

EXERCISE

Look back at your note groups to see if you can find any topics that are difficult to express concisely. If you find any topics, write them below or on some note paper.

Use plain English and concise, active language to reduce these topics to just the essential information.

_____

_____

_____

_____

_____

_____

_____

_____

_____

_____

_____

_____

AVOID JARGON AND UNNECESSARY SPECIALTY TERMS

Ask yourself what levels of technical knowledge your listeners have. If some listeners have limited technical understanding, then you might need to be especially careful to use plain English to describe any technical topics you address.

There are several ways to remind yourself what terms may be hard for others to understand. If you talk about your work with people outside your field, then try to identify ideas that tend to puzzle them. Or try to remember your own professional growth — thinking back to a time before you had learned technical terminology that you're familiar with now. Think about what aspect of a new term, or a new professional object or process, was difficult for you to understand once.

These processes can help you identify jargon and specialty terms that might confuse your listeners. These three steps can prevent you from losing your audience with language that's too complicated for them:

- Make sure you're ready to use plain English to define any terms that audience members may not know. This step will help people learn from what you say and follow your ideas.
- Engage the audience when your language gets more complicated by asking how many people know an unusual term.
- Step back and provide more context whenever your listeners look puzzled.

EXERCISE

Look back at your note groups to see if you can find any topics that involve specialty terms that might confuse some members of your audience. Use this space or some note paper to list ways you can use plain English and context explanations to make complicated terms easy to grasp.

_____

_____

_____

_____

_____

_____

Add visuals and imagery that suit your audience and enhance your content

Even talented public speakers rely on visuals and metaphorical imagery to add variety to their presentations. Here are some planning tips on how to integrate visuals and imagery into the speech you're planning.

One tip applies to all these slide elements: always engage the audience and not the slide! It insults your listeners any time you forget them and become fascinated with an intricate chart you've created.

Learn your content beforehand. Then devote your time and energy to using visual slide elements to help the audience members grasp your ideas as clearly as you do.

USE TEXT-BASED VISUALS: LISTS AND TABLES

Information becomes more difficult to absorb the longer your sentences and paragraphs are. That's one reason it's risky to include a lot of sentences and paragraphs in your presentation slides.

As you'll notice in this workbook, lists break up information into bite-size chunks. It's easier to grasp a speaker's logic in a list because the format accomplishes several tasks:

- Identifies a theme that a few items share
- Separates items from one another
- Makes it easy to skim text quickly

Tables also introduce clean visual lines of separation between distinct ideas. Labeled rows and columns are especially good ways to present quantitative facts to listeners.

Make sure any list or table relates clearly to the theme and topic it appears under. Strip away as much unnecessary text and as many unnecessary figures as you can. If a visual element must be complex, then add a few arrows to highlight what's most important.

Lists and charts can provide a welcome break for you as a speaker, and they provide a change of pace for the audience. But they should never flood audience members with too much text or data.

USE DATA-BASED VISUALS: CHARTS

Charts make quantitative data clear, and they take different forms:

- Pie charts and ring charts (at right) for percentages
- Line charts
- Area charts (such as the 2010–2011 chart below)
- Bar charts

Whatever form best suits your numeric data, keep your design simple. (The 2010–2011 area chart is almost as simple as a chart can get.) If you're concerned that a chart may deepen complexity without enhancing clarity, then either look for ways to simplify the chart or consider leaving it out.

USE IMAGERY

Charts and tables are likely to be better suited to an audience whose members are comfortable with math. Lists may be better suited to social scientists who want to know what unites and divides a set of items. And imagery may be more appropriate for a literary or creative audience.

2013   2014

490K

306K

NUMBER OF
CONTAINERS

Your audience members may be likely to respond intuitively to imagery. In that case, think of how a quotation, a metaphor, or a simile might bring one of your ideas to life. For instance, a clothing company might use buttons to symbolize quarterly sales by plotting four round button dots on a line chart.

Don't limit your thinking. Lines of poetry might be appropriate for a presentation on industrial chemistry, while a group of novelists with one publisher might appreciate seeing a chart of changes in their combined annual sales.

The most important aspect of all visuals and images is that they must help your listeners grasp your ideas. If you're in doubt about whether an image adds clarity, then ask a colleague for a second opinion — especially a colleague who's new to your topic.

EXERCISE

Look back at your themes and note groups to see what topics lend themselves to text-based visuals, data-based visuals, and metaphorical imagery. Use this space or some note paper to say how you'll use visuals and/or imagery to add color to your presentation. Or draw a sketch of visual elements you could include.

_____

_____

_____

_____

_____

_____

_____

_____

_____

_____

Step 5. Plan an in-person or virtual presentation

Build in times to engage the audience directly

Try to engage the audience every few minutes. Here are some strategies:

- "Let's have a show of hands. How many of you have had this experience …?"
- "I could address either of two topics here. Let's vote on which one."
- "How many of you are familiar with [Topic X]?"

Watching a presentation should not be like watching TV. Moments of engagement help your audience members actively participate in the event you've planned. Frequent, planned moments of engagement help hold listeners' interest and keep them invested in what you have to say.

EXERCISE

Examine your agenda, themes, and most important ideas. Ask yourself what kinds of questions, quizzes, or group activities might help clarify your ideas and themes.

List some engaging activities, and spell out how they relate to your purpose and key sentence.

_____

_____

_____

_____

_____

_____

_____

_____

_____

_____

_____

Structure your agendas, breaks, Q&A sessions, and conclusions

You'll practice your presentation in Part Two, but time management should be part of your planning process from the beginning. Start with an intuitive sense of how much material you have and how well it fits your total timeframe.

As you practice your delivery in Part Two, be ready to return to the planning process to change the length of your presentation in two ways:

- Either to further reduce and streamline your ideas
- Or to fill them out — e.g., with activities to engage your audience, or with additional groups of notes

Make sure you leave time for one or more question-and-answer (Q&A) sessions to boost engagement. Q&A sessions help you achieve these three aims:

- Boost credibility
- Test whether the audience understands and accepts key points
- Provide an opportunity to fill in information gaps

Also include final slides for your presentation's summary or conclusion, or next steps that someone will take:

- If your goal is to INFORM the audience, then it's important to include a summary slide to remind them of your most important information.

- You can also include a summary slide if your goal is to PERSUADE the audience. For these presentations, you should always include a conclusion slide, next-steps slide, or both so that your audience knows what you want them to do.

Decide what kind of topics you might propose for one or more Q&A sessions. List the topics here.

_____

_____

_____

_____

_____

_____

_____

_____

_____

Also decide how summary or conclusion slides can wrap up your presentation. How could these slides strengthen your presentation's central purpose — to inform, or to persuade?

_____

_____

_____

_____

_____

_____

_____

_____

_____

Plan a virtual presentation

Webinars and other online presentations enable you to reach people who aren't gathered in one location. If you record the presentation, listeners may see and hear you at another time. If they can download all handouts, you'll eliminate printing costs. Freedom from those physical constraints means that you may be able to reach many more people online than in a building.

Here's a checklist to help you prepare a virtual presentation that won't rely on eye contact or body language to convey a sense that you're present for your audience members:

☐ **MAKE SURE YOUR PRESENTATION INCLUDES FREQUENT OPPORTUNITIES FOR ENGAGEMENT.** You'll learn more about asking and answering questions in Part Two. The main planning idea to keep in mind from the start is to build in many chances to find out what your audience members are thinking, and give them chances to interact with your ideas.

☐ **MAKE SURE THE INTERFACE WILL FUNCTION SMOOTHLY.** You may need help navigating the demands of an idiosyncratic Web interface. If so, hire a professional service based on the audio, video, recording, and interactive features that best suit your content. Online polls and quizzes are two examples of interactivity.

☐ **MAKE SURE ALL THE PUZZLE PIECES FIT TOGETHER.** Your presentation may involve juggling animations or video. If it does, make sure you carefully coordinate them with your speaking topics. Practice thoroughly beforehand to make sure all your resources are in place and working smoothly.

☐ **CONSIDER HIRING EXPERTS TO HELP YOU PROMOTE A VIRTUAL PRESENTATION** — for instance, through social media. Promoters may be able to advise you how to use other media, e.g., Twitter, to boost audience engagement.

HELP LISTENERS UNDERSTAND YOUR ORGANIZATION

Organizations can benefit immensely when employees are able to explain the organization's work to larger audiences in an engaging way. Successful in-person, online, and on-camera presentations can be great demonstrations of present or future leadership skills. s.

Pause a moment to take stock of everything you've accomplished in Part One. You've already answered half the questions that might have made you nervous at the outset:

- Who am I speaking to?
- Why am I speaking in the first place?
- How should I articulate all my ideas?
- How do I organize [X] minutes' or hours' worth of thoughts?
- How do I interact with the audience to really involve them in what I'm saying?

Coming up in Part Two, you'll learn techniques to use your voice, hands, and body language effectively. You'll also learn ways to pose and answer questions in ways that keep audience members engaged.

You'll practice various delivery methods and use rehearsals to pull together all your planning and delivery techniques. Then you'll be in excellent shape on the day your presentation is scheduled.

PART TWO:
DELIVER YOUR PRESENTATION

Objectives

In Part One you developed a thorough plan for a presentation. That plan will now be clear in your mind, and it will help you share clear ideas with your audience.

You'll find that the plan you've developed will also help you decide how you'll deliver your presentation. Consciously planning and practicing your delivery will make you a much more effective communicator the day you give your presentation.

Here are some of the challenges you'll master in Part Two:

- Convey confidence, sensitivity, attentiveness, and authority
- Find effective ways to use your voice and your body language
- Practice projecting a confident, professional image
- Practice engaging the audience and helping them grasp your main message

All these actions will help you grasp the mechanics of your presentation. You'll transform your presentation from a set of well-planned ideas into a vocal, physical, well-timed performance.

Planning your ideas and your delivery gives you a reliable framework that you've tested beforehand:

- You'll stay focused on your ideas
- Your audience will follow your presentation plan
- And your ideas will stay clear in everyone's minds throughout your delivery

Here are the five steps to practice, rehearse, and deliver your presentation:

- Step 1. Practice your speaking
- Step 2. Practice your eye contact
- Step 3. Practice your expressions and movement
- Step 4. Practice asking and answering questions
- Step 5. Pull everything together through rehearsals

You'll find explanations of each step below.

Step 1. Practice your speaking

Your voice is the foundation of any presentation you deliver. If your presentation is online, it's especially important to be aware of your vocal presence. The steps below will help you use your voice consciously, as a tool to help your listeners follow your ideas.

We'll use the words *practice* and *rehearsal* differently in this book:

- **PRACTICING** your presentation is a discovery process. You practice to discover different ways you *might* look and sound as you speak. (For instance, practicing might include trying out a range of speaking volumes.)
- In contrast, a **REHEARSAL** is an effort to duplicate how you *will* speak and carry yourself the day of your presentation. (For instance, rehearsal might involve meeting a colleague in an auditorium you'll present in, and asking if you're clearly audible in the back of the room.)

We'll get to the final step of rehearsal at the end of Part Two.

Practice your breathing, volume, pitch, and vocal tone

Your voice is a wind instrument. Practicing the following three techniques will improve its clarity.

PRACTICE DIAPHRAGMATIC BREATHING:

- Stand with your feet one foot apart
- Place your hand above your navel
- Inhale deeply — feeling your stomach expand — and try to yawn or smile
- Exhale completely — saying "Ahhh" as you do

MODULATE YOUR VOLUME:

- Practice delivering part of your presentation
- Listen to how you sound as you speak
- Ask others to listen, and ask them if your voice is too soft or loud
- Purposely vary your volume, looking for the best match for the room where you'll deliver your presentation

LOWER YOUR PITCH:

- First, find your natural pitch — your humming and speaking voice should match
- Then speak from your diaphragm

These three techniques will help your audience hear you clearly.

Experiment with your vocal tone

Here's an exercise to help you understand your vocal tone and explore how powerfully it shapes the ways you sound.

EXERCISE

Try repeating this sentence several times, stressing a different word each time:

"I didn't say she bit the dog."

There are three important points to note:

- Note how much your meaning can change when you emphasize a single different word.
- Note how strongly your emphasis can alter the tone of what you say.
- Finally, note that trying to write a script for yourself can blind you to this change in tone. Namely, a script can focus your attention on a specific word order — instead of how your listeners will perceive your vocal tone.

Below, you'll practice different aspects of your presentation and then rehearse the whole thing. As you practice and rehearse, track how your emphasis feels more effective or less effective when you experiment with your vocal tone.

Exaggerate your enunciation

It's important to speak clearly so that your audience members can follow along. Exaggerating your enunciation by speaking syllables more distinctly will help your listeners grasp each idea you discuss.

Here are two enunciation tips:

- Pay special attention to the consonants *T, D, C, G, M, N, P, B, L,* and *R.*
- Time yourself so that you speak about 150 words per minute. Speaking more quickly makes enunciation difficult.

Test how your voice sounds online or in a room

Test the equipment you'll use on the day of your presentation to make sure you know how to operate it and make sure it's working correctly.

Also test how your clothing appears on-screen. Patterns are usually distracting and certain colors, such as red, don't transmit well. It's better to wear muted colors.

For any virtual presentation, remember that your voice is your single most powerful physical delivery tool. Be sure to enunciate, pause, and speak across a good vocal range.

EXERCISE

Call your own phone, and practice delivering part of your presentation. Then call your voicemail to listen to how your voice sounds.

Using your phone gives you a valuable, audio-only sense of what kind of presence your voice is projecting. If you try this exercise with video, you might immediately get distracted by some aspect of how you look and how you move. We'll get to those points later! For now, just focus on how you sound.

Come back and repeat this exercise, asking yourself these questions:

- How do I actually sound on voicemail, compared to how I imagined I'd sound?
- How does my delivery improve as I repeat this practice for my content?

EXERCISE

It's very difficult for an audience member to stay attentive if you speak in a monotone. The following exercise is especially useful if your topic seems dull to you, or if you're afraid your topic won't be interesting for your audience.

Here's the process:

- Find a book for preschool children, and make an audio recording of yourself reading it.
- Now record yourself delivering the most familiar part of your presentation in the same way — as if you were trying to fascinate and wow a group of little kids at story time.

This exercise may feel especially silly at first if your presentation is about a very serious topic, such as an obscure detail of maritime taxes. However, the drier the professional topic is, the more helpful the exercise will be.

This exercise has several benefits:

- It helps you listen to the full range of tones, pitches, and volumes that you draw on to make the children's book sound vivid.
- It prepares you to branch out into a wider range of tones, pitches, and volumes as you turn back to your own presentation topic.
- Finally, if you're carefully preparing to speak about obscure details of maritime taxation, then you deserve to have some fun in the process!

Step 2. Practice your eye contact

Establishing eye contact with audience members in a non-virtual presentation will help you establish a good rapport with them. Eye contact is an in-person follow-up to the effort you made in Part One to identify and understand your audience.

Eye contact signals several things about you, e.g., …

- Confidence
- Trustworthiness
- Gratitude for audience members' attention
- Readiness to pay attention to them in return

Eye contact helps emphasize the fact that a professional presentation involves your *receiving and evaluating* information, as well as just *providing* information.

Maintain eye contact

You don't need to think about eye contact if you're leading a webinar. But if you're in a room with people, don't look at the floor, walls, or ceiling during your presentation, and don't stare out the window.

Remember that any presentation is an interpersonal event. Neglecting your eye contact can make you seem insecure, evasive, or disengaged. However, maintaining good eye contact will help you convey confidence, authority, attentiveness, and respect for your listeners' time and attention.

Practice sweeping your eyes across a crowd at a measured rate

Think of your eyes as being like a second hand ticking around the circumference of an old-fashioned clock:

- Maintain eye contact with each person for about two to five seconds
- Move from left to right and from right to left across all the people in front of you or around you
- Don't show any bias for or against particular audience members
- Look *at* your listeners — not *through* them

Practice all these techniques — for instance, by envisioning your future audience as you stand in an empty room. This kind of practice will help you maintain a good visual rapport with the people who'll show up to see and hear what you have to say.

Step 3. Practice your expressions and movement

Effective expressions, gestures, and movement can make the difference between a good presentation and a great presentation.

It's difficult for words to convey how you should move effectively or how you should look. That's why practice and rehearsal are especially important to find physical movement that translates into effective communication.

This section suggests several ways you can practice how you'll look as you speak.

Practice your facial expressions and hand gestures

Here are five general guidelines for what expressions and hand and arm gestures can make you a more effective speaker:

- **PRACTICE HOW YOUR HAND AND ARM MOVEMENTS CAN ECHO AND ENHANCE YOUR IDEAS:**

  - To clarify or demonstrate (e.g., by using your hands to indicate "Here's something new in front of me" when you present a substantial new idea)

  - To compare and contrast information (e.g., by using a literal "On the one hand; on the other hand" paired set of gestures)

  - To count off points under a theme (e.g., by using your fingers to match a slide with a list by ticking off each item with one finger "Here are four related points. Point One …. Point Two …. Point Three ….")

- **PRACTICE OCCUPYING SPACE** (e.g., a large room, small room, or shared table) the way you will when you deliver the presentation. Explore different gestures that feel right for the ideas and themes you've planned.

- **SMILE OFTEN** — balancing friendly attention with professionalism.

- **USE YOUR EYEBROWS TO DRAMATIZE WORDS AND IDEAS,** but suit your expressions to your content. (E.g., don't smile during a solemn topic.)

- **REMEMBER THAT YOU'VE ALREADY PRACTICED THE MOST IMPORTANT FACIAL MOVEMENT:** maintaining effective eye contact.

Finally, here are three rules of thumb to keep in mind as you try out different expressions and hand and arm gestures to keep your audience engaged:

- Avoid too much repetition — especially if it feels mechanical.
- Aim for expressions and movements that feel natural rather than forced.
- Try for expressions and movements that feel spontaneous rather than intentional.

Practice your body language

Your body language is always conveying something — especially when you have a room's attention. Here are some general descriptions that can help you maintain a positive physical presence as you speak professionally:

- If you'll stand for the presentation, then practice walking around and occasionally changing your standing position.

- Don't move restlessly: instead, practice occupying the space as your rightful spot, for the full time that you'll be sharing ideas that matter.

- Practice holding your posture to balance opposing factors:

    - Looking assertive without being aggressive
    - Looking professional without being rigid

- Practice nodding frequently to show interest in what audience members will say in the Q&A sessions you'll plan.

It can feel awkward to practice gestures. But in your conversations, you almost certainly do gesture naturally when you're clarifying or emphasizing a point, or contrasting two ideas. Practicing your gestures in a business context may feel awkward, but it looks (and actually is) a very natural thing to do!

If you feel awkward practicing your gestures, imagine delivering your presentation to an amazingly sympathetic person who's eager to hear you explain each aspect of your topic. Use your computer, phone, or camcorder to record video of yourself as you engage in this imaginary discussion with a sympathetic, engaged listener.

Watch the recording, and note what works. Add the effective gestures to your professional "vocabulary" of body language that helps you look professional and helps make your ideas concrete and clear.

Also be aware of your audience members' body language, and be ready to fine-tune your own body language and speaking style responsively.

Is the listener ...	Body language
Concentrating?	• Leans forward • Strokes chin
Bored or tired?	• Yawns • Removes glasses and puts them down • Looks at phone or types
Confused?	Scowls
Annoyed?	Avoids eye contact

Here are a few fine-tuning responses you can practice:

- Imagine listeners seeming to concentrate or looking confused. Practice slowing down to help them keep up.
- Imagine that people are yawning. Try using a wider range of vocal tone to hold their attention.
- Imagine that people seem annoyed. Aim for an especially respectful tone that also maintains your self-respect.

EXERCISE

Use your computer, phone, or camcorder to record video of yourself as you practice sections of your presentation:

- Evaluate your eye contact, expressions, body language, and voice.
- Look for patterns that effectively match your themes and purpose.
- Look for new patterns you want to change.
- Notice your improvements over time.

As you practice on video, you get closer to being ready for a full rehearsal: the time when you pull together all the various aspects of your presentation into one successful whole.

Step 4. Practice asking and answering questions

You already considered several important questions about the audience in Part One. Now it's time to consider framing questions for audience members and prepare to reply to questions they'll ask.

This step brings us back to one of the keys of an effective presentation: that you should always remember your audience — keeping in mind that you're there to *exchange* messages with them.

Effective presenters don't see audience members as blank slates to write on. The most effective presentations are activities that the presenter and audience engage in with one another — cooperatively reaching a shared understanding.

Plan the questions you'll ask: the P3 technique

You should ask your audience questions to keep them engaged. Here's a three-step process, the P3 technique:

1. **POSE** a question
2. **PAUSE** for a moment — giving listeners a chance to think
3. **PICK** someone to reply

Try to harness all your questions to the presentation plan that you developed in Part One. Try to relate each question you ask to underlying aspects of the presentation structure you've developed, such as these:

- Your key sentence
- Your central purpose
- Your overarching themes

This close coordination between your presentation plan and your delivery will help you feel confident and prepared. Coordinating your planning with your delivery will also help you engage your audience.

EXERCISE

Use the space below or some note paper to list a set of questions that fit each of the three or four major themes of your presentation. Avoid open-ended questions: sparking and managing discussions is a demanding skill of its own. Frame questions for this exercise to elicit short, specific answers.

_____

_____

_____

_____

_____

_____

_____

_____

_____

Practice how you'll carry yourself in Q&A sessions

Encourage your audience members to ask you questions — a process that helps keep them engaged. Here's a seven-point checklist for any Q&A session:

- ☐ Thank people who ask you questions
- ☐ Stand or lean closer to the audience during Q&A than when you were speaking
- ☐ Use open-hand gestures
- ☐ Repeat the question when the group is large
- ☐ Paraphrase the question if it's long or hard to understand
- ☐ Answer clearly and concisely
- ☐ Pause after you answer, to allow follow-up questions

And here are four things *not* to do during a Q&A session:

- ☐ Ask, "Did that answer your question?"
- ☐ Use ambiguous words such as *maybe*, *perhaps*, or *probably*
- ☐ Use negative body language — e.g., shaking your head, slumping, or looking down
- ☐ Look only at a person who's just asked a question

If your answer to any question becomes especially complex, take a second or two to look around the audience after every few sentences.

Maintaining eye contact with other audience members will help tell you whether everyone is following the information that was sparked by one listener's question. This eye contact shows that you're still listening to and looking at your audience as a whole.

Plan to encourage questions, and practice answering them

Start this planning process by brainstorming about the questions that you can imagine growing naturally from the ideas you'll state. Then practice these actions:

- Paraphrasing the question
- Answering concisely
- Answering with an illustration
- Responding to questioners who have different moods and approaches

Remind yourself that you may always get unexpected questions. If you do, avoid responding by saying, "I don't know." Instead, say, "I'll find out."

You can also use the SPAR strategy to frame your response — choosing one of these four options based on each question you get:

- **SITUATION:** "Here's the situation"; "Here are the facts"; "Here are the circumstances"

- **PROPOSAL:** "This is what I propose"; "This is what I can do"; "This is what I suggest"

- **ACTION:** "I'll be sure to"; "I can"; "I'll follow up on that by"

- **REASON:** "The reason is"; "This is why that will work"

EXERCISE

1. Imagine several likely questions that your audience will have, and practice answering them.

2. Write out your questions on notes, and pick two notes to address at once. Use these notes to practice how you'd handle answering two questions that an audience member asked at the same time.

3. Imagine at least one unlikely question, and use the SPAR strategy to practice answering it.

EXERCISE

Use the space below or some note paper to list questions for your audience members that fit each of the three or four major themes of your presentation.

_____

_____

_____

_____

_____

_____

_____

_____

_____

_____

_____

_____

_____

_____

_____

_____

_____

_____

_____

_____

_____

Step 5. Pull everything together through rehearsals

As we noted on page 40, practicing and rehearsing are two different phases of preparation:

- **Practicing** is a process to discover different ways you *might* look and sound as you speak
- **Rehearsal** is an effort to duplicate how you *will* speak and carry yourself the day of your presentation

Practicing is like the brainstorming process in Part One when you wrote out notes that you might or might not use — just to keep your ideas flowing. Practicing helps you explore different aspects of your presentation by letting possible situations and responses flow past you.

Rehearsal is a later, bigger process. In rehearsals, you start pulling together all the aspects of your presentation — the ideas and themes, the Q&A times, and the ways you'll sound and look as you speak.

Rehearsals weave together any rough edges that remain between all these presentation elements — shaping a complex communication event into one familiar, well-planned, seamless whole. The more thoroughly you rehearse, the more natural and successful your final presentation is likely to feel.

Plan how you'll incorporate handouts

If you'll include any handouts, be sure to rehearse how you'll use them. Be ready to take these three steps:

- Let the audience know at the start whether a handout will make it unnecessary for them to take notes
- Distribute a handout only when you're ready to address its topic
- Give any instructions right away (e.g., "Please pass these around the table" or "Please turn to page 2")

Consider sharing your handouts only *after* your presentation. Otherwise, some participants may opt out of listening to you, dive in to the materials you give them, and try to start teaching themselves.

Practice guiding your listeners through your points — ensuring that they never feel lost

Remember the first two steps of Part One: identify your audience, and identify your most important messages. Keep those principles in mind as you rehearse your presentation delivery.

There's a fine balance to strike in most presentations:

- On the one hand, you want audience members to be engaged
- But on the other hand, you want to offer them a clear program that's perfectly easy to follow

Your main role is as a guide for your audience, as they travel through terrain that you've carefully mapped out for them. Remember that your audience members' path will probably be different from yours. To arrive at your presentation topic, you may have blazed a fascinating trail through a host of serious business challenges:

- Conducting painstaking **research**
- Untangling **concepts that defied easy analysis**

Those processes may have been difficult and exciting for you. And it can be very effective when a speaker conveys intellectual excitement and struggle in describing a business topic. However, as a presenter, your job is to chart a course that's so smooth and clear, the audience members can follow you almost effortlessly.

LEAD YOUR AUDIENCE BY FOLLOWING YOUR PRESENTATION PLAN

Think of each presentation as a cycle of following and leadership:

- You **are following** your presentation plan as you practice your delivery
- You **will follow** your delivery plan on the day of your presentation
- And this process should make it easy for your listeners **to follow you**

In other words, a presentation calls on you take on some roles and responsibilities of leadership — providing clear guidance to a number of other professional people. But you'll still have the comfort of following a presentation plan that you've very carefully developed beforehand.

The following three steps can transform your hard preparatory work into benefits that an audience will grasp easily:

- **SHARE THE FRUITS OF YOUR RESEARCH.** Present your findings first, without leaving the audience in suspense about what you found. Only discuss difficult research procedures if they're relevant to your listeners' questions.

- **CHALLENGE YOURSELF TO PAINT A VERY CLEAR PICTURE FOR YOUR LISTENERS.** Start with a clear point right away, each and every time you start discussing a new theme. Then provide further explanatory detail.

- **PROVE YOUR ANALYTICAL SKILLS BY SPEAKING VERY CONCISELY AND CLEARLY.** Reduce complex information to simple underlying structures and logical sequences. Then everyone will be able to see plainly — thanks to your prior analytical effort, delivered in plain English.

Careful planning and practice can help you minimize the risks of your audience members' feeling lost or confused. The result should be a well-plotted sightseeing tour of a sequence of ideas. Provide enough context to keep all your audience members feeling engaged and enlightened from start to finish.

Manage the time you'll need
and the time your audience will need

By the rehearsal phase, you're ready to juggle the themes, Q&A sessions, handout management, and all other details of your presentation — all while keeping an eye on the clock.

Review the five-step plan for Part One and the first four steps you've just completed for Part Two. Check that each necessary element is in place, and conduct a full rehearsal of the presentation. Include time that your audience members will need to speak or to think.

Return to Part One for any fine-tuning or substantive overhauling you need to do to stay on time. Revisiting Part One, Step 4 should be especially helpful (see pages 24–33):

- Reorganizing your notes can help you identify dead wood that there's room to cut
- Reorganization can also suggest new opportunities to expand on ideas in beneficial detail

Your presentation will be much stronger when you scale your content to closely match your time. And your connection with your audience will be stronger when they can trust you to respect their time along with their attention.

Practice transitioning back to your most important point

This last idea is simple: don't lose sight of your main point! And don't let your audience members walk away without a clear return to the point you prepared them to understand, right from the start.

As you rehearse, remember that it's helpful to rephrase your key sentence in different ways. Look for ways to use your presentation themes and more minor ideas to support your main idea.

Here are three times when it can be especially helpful to state or return to your key sentence — especially in a longer presentation:

- State your key sentence and explain your main point very early in the presentation — as soon as you can lay down enough context for the listeners to understand it
- Restate the key sentence as you transition from one major theme to another, elaborating on it or reframing it as your ideas expand
- And consider restating your key sentence whenever an audience member's question takes the discussion off course — gathering everyone's attention again so that you can all move together toward a final, shared conclusion

Returning to your key sentence and main point at the end should give you and your listeners a satisfying sense of completion. Practice using your vocal tone and pacing to convey a sense that your presentation has now successfully wound down.

CONGRATULATIONS!

That's the conclusion of Write It Well's ten-step process to develop and deliver an effective presentation.

In Part One, you carefully mapped out a landscape of ideas and planned how you'd help your audience members travel through that landscape with you.

In Part Two, you consciously drew on your voice, hands, and body language as tools to help your audience follow along. You also planned how you'll invite questions and pose questions to audience members so that they can better understand the terrain you'll travel together.

Rehearsals will give you the time you need to bring together all these communication tasks into a single successful journey.

Best wishes for the successful presentation that you're now ready to deliver.

About Write It Well

Write It Well began in 1979 as Advanced Communication Designs, Inc. We're a firm of trainers and professional-development consultants who help people in business communicate more efficiently and effectively.

We provide practical, job-relevant information, techniques, and strategies that readers and training participants can apply right away to the documents they produce and presentations they deliver for their jobs. Individuals, teams, training specialists, instructors in corporations and businesses of all sizes, nonprofit organizations, government agencies, and colleges and universities use our books and training programs.

The Write It Well Series on Business Communication includes the self-paced training workbooks *Professional Writing Skills*; *Effective Email*; *Land the Job: Writing Effective Resumes and Cover Letters*; *Reports, Proposals, and Procedures*; and *Writing Performance Reviews*. Visit writeitwell.com for more information about our company and detailed descriptions of our publications.

About the author

Natasha Terk is the author of *Reports, Proposals, and Procedures*; *Professional Writing Skills*; *Land the Job: Writing Effective Resumes and Cover Letters*; *Effective Email: Concise, Clear Writing to Advance Your Business Needs*; and *Writing Performance Reviews*. As the managing director of Write It Well, she leads the firm's business operations and strategy.

Natasha holds master's degrees from the University of San Francisco and the University of Manchester, UK. She has served as a program officer at the Packard Foundation and as a management consultant with La Piana Consulting, and she serves on the board of the Ronald McDonald House of San Francisco.

Natasha has taught business writing at the University of California, Berkeley, and been a consultant for Berkeley's Haas School of Business. She leads on-site and online webinars and workshops for clients including Hewlett-Packard, Granite Construction, IKEA, National Semiconductor, and the Port of Oakland. She gives keynote speeches and presentations on business communications at seminars and large conferences.